the legend of the

Curse

of the

BAMBINO

Dan Shaughnessy
illustrated by C. F. Payne

A Paula Wiseman Book
Simon & Schuster Books for Young Readers
New York   London   Toronto   Sydney

The day had finally come—the opening day of baseball season—and Kate couldn't wait. Dad had season tickets, the same seats Grandpa had had back in the old days. Everyone in the family was a Red Sox fan, and each year Dad took one of the children to the first game. It was finally Kate's turn. Kate had never been to Fenway Park before, and on this opening day the Sox were playing the New York Yankees.

Kate knew she would sit in a place where her dad, granddad, and great-granddad had watched their favorite team. She imagined them sitting in these very same seats, cracking open peanuts and spilling the shells onto the concrete floor below.

"Dad, who was the greatest ballplayer who ever lived?" she asked.

"That's easy, Kate," her dad said. "It was George Herman Ruth, the great Bambino. The Babe. The Sultan of Swat. The Colossus of Clout. He was the best pitcher—then he was the best hitter. He had it all, and some think he's still part of the game."

"Does he still play baseball?" Kate asked.

"No, not since Great-Granddad's time, and there was never another like him. But his spirit watches over the Red Sox, especially any time they are playing the Yankees."

"Why them?"

"Well, Kate," Dad continued, "the Babe started playing with the Red Sox when he was only a teenager, and they won the World Series three times while he was in Boston. Once the Babe left Boston, the Red Sox didn't win again for more than eighty years. Some people thought the Red Sox were jinxed because of his trade to the Yankees. That's what some call 'the Curse of the Bambino.' Great-Granddad was here at Fenway when the Babe won it with the Sox, and he used to tell me about it. . . ."

It was a gray Monday afternoon, September 9, 1918. The World Series was being played earlier than usual because of war overseas. It was the Red Sox versus the Cubs. The Red Sox, led by their young, stout lefty pitcher, Babe Ruth, had been champions of the world in 1915 and 1916 and had never lost a World Series. Now the Babe gave them a great chance to win again. Though he was Boston's best pitcher, the Babe also led the league in homers and could beat the Cubs with his bat.

When the Series moved into Fenway Park, Boston led the Cubs, two games to one, and needed only two more victories to clinch the championship. At the start of Game Four the great Bambino was working on a World Series shutout streak of twenty-three straight scoreless innings. It had rained a few hours before the game, and Great-Granddad told me he sat on his newspaper to keep his pants dry while he watched from the right-field stands.

It was scoreless in the bottom of the fourth, but the Red Sox were threatening. They had two runners on base with two outs. Up next was the mighty Babe. Even though he was pitching most of the time, the Babe had walloped eleven homers in 1918 and was the most powerful hitter on the Red Sox.

Gripping his bat tightly as he walked toward home plate, the Babe muttered to himself, "I'll take care of these National League bums."

A roar went up in the Fenway stands when fans saw the Babe stepping up to the plate.

"Hit it out, Babe!" they yelled.

"Win your own game!" some shouted.

"You can do it, Babe!" other fans cheered.

The park went quiet as Cubs pitcher Lefty Tyler threw ball one, ball two, then ball three. The next two pitches were strikes. Then Lefty took his last windup.

Fans were standing and cheering when Tyler threw again, and this time the Babe unleashed a ferocious swing, swatting the ball high and far over the head of the Cubs' right fielder. The Babe wasn't the fastest of runners, but his blast carried so far that both runners were able to score and the Babe made it to third base for a triple.

On the strength of his bat and his arm, the Babe was the winning pitcher for the Red Sox that day, and the Sox led the Series, three games to one. Two days after the Babe's big win, Boston finished off the Cubs to win the World Series for a record fifth time. The Sox were the dominant team in baseball, and they had the best player, Babe Ruth. Fans filing out of Fenway Park thought their string of championships might never end.

But just one season after that last World Series win, the Red Sox sold Babe Ruth to the New York Yankees for cash. And it seemed that all of Boston's good luck went to New York with the great Bambino. The Yankees went on to win twenty-six World Series in Yankee Stadium, a new park that became known as "the House That Ruth Built."

While the Yankees kept winning championships, the Red Sox could only come close. They seemed to have the worst luck in baseball, and over time some people started to wonder if the team was cursed.

★ ★ ★ Special Boston News. ★ ★ ★

October 15, 1946. ST. LOUIS—The St. Louis Cardinals defeated the heavily favored Boston Red Sox in the seventh game of the World Series today. As Boston shortstop Johnny Pesky hesitated with a relay throw from center field, Enos Slaughter galloped around the bases with the winning run.

★ ★ ★ ★ ★ ★ ★ ★ ★ ★ ★ ★

And sometimes the strangest things would happen to the Red Sox.

50 Cents

Monday, October 2, 1978

Sox Home for the Winter

New York Sports Special

October 2, 1978. BOSTON—Bucky Dent's pop-fly home run into the screen over Fenway's left-field wall was the key blow as the Yankees defeated the Red Sox, 5–4, in a one-game play-off at Fenway Park. Dent, a weak-hitting shortstop, managed only four home runs during the season, but it was his blast that propelled the Yankees to victory and sent the Sox home for the winter.

17

When it came to the Red Sox in the big game, no lead was ever safe.

Red Sox Denied

October 25, 1986. NEW YORK—Mookie Wilson's ground ball dribbled between the legs of Red Sox first baseman Bill Buckner, denying the Sox their first World Series win in 68 years. The Sox were one strike away from a Series victory over the Mets at Shea Stadium when the New Yorkers staged an improbable two-out, three-run rally to win Game Six.

And the Yankees always seemed to be coming out on top.

SPORTS

YANKEES COMEBACK

October 16, 2003. NEW YORK—Aaron Boone's eleventh-inning home run capped a dramatic Yankees comeback and pushed the Yankees past the Red Sox, 6–5, in the seventh and final game of the American League Championship Series. The Red Sox led Game Seven, 5–2, in the eighth inning when ace pitcher Pedro Martinez got tired and was left on the mound by Sox manager Grady Little.

But then came the magical season of 2004, when the Red Sox beat the Yankees, won the World Series, and lifted the Curse of the Bambino forever.

Sox Victorious

October 20, 2004. NEW YORK—After losing the first three games of the American League Championship Series, the Red Sox made history by coming back to beat the Yankees four straight times. Johnny Damon's grand slam clinched Boston's 10–3 win in Game Seven.

The Curse Reversed

October 27, 2004. ST. LOUIS—Under a full red moon caused by a lunar eclipse, the Red Sox beat the St. Louis Cardinals, 3–0, completing a four-game sweep and delivering a World Series championship to Boston for the first time in 86 years.

"Dad," Kate asked, "did you ever believe in the Curse of the Bambino?"

"No, sweetie, I don't think the Babe would have ever done something like that.

"There was always hope for the Red Sox. It's like Great-Granddad said—you've got to believe in believing. And never give up on your team. I think the spirit of the Babe was always with the Red Sox. And always will be."

For Marilou, Sarah, Kate, and Sam—D. S.

I would like to thank my family for their love and support,
for without it this book would not be possible.—C. F. P.

Afterword

Fathers and daughters. Mothers and sons. Grandparents and grandkids. It is through family that most of us are introduced to baseball and ballparks, and it is the connection of generations that sustains a love of baseball, especially in championship-starved New England. When the Red Sox finally won the World Series in 2004, there were few living souls who could remember Boston's last championship in 1918. The end of the long quest rewarded the eternal faith and loyalty of Red Sox fans. The Red Sox never go out of season or out of style, and they furnish post-game debate and hot-stove chatter for twelve months of every year. Other teams have fans, but only the Red Sox have spawned a Nation. There have been heartbreaks since Ruth was sold after the 1919 season. Since the sale of the Babe, the Yankees have led the Sox in championships by a count of 26–1, and in that time the Sox have lost four World Series in Game Seven and two one-game play-offs—not to mention an excruciating loss in the 2003 American League Championship Series, when victory over the Yankees finally seemed secure. But the Curse of the Bambino was broken once and for all by the 2004 Red Sox, a true storybook team.

Bibliography

Boston Globe, September 9, 1918, "Ruth-Tyler Likely in Game Here Today"; September 10, 1918, "Keeping Ruth Hitless Too Big a Job Even for 'Lefty' Tyler"; September 10, 1918, "Sox Win on Wild Chuck to Merkle"; September 11, 1918, "Sox Win Championship"; September 12, 1918, "Red Sox Win Sixth Game and the Title"; September 12, 1918, "Red Sox, World's Baseball Champions for 1918."

SIMON & SCHUSTER BOOKS FOR YOUNG READERS • An imprint of Simon & Schuster Children's Publishing Division, 1230 Avenue of the Americas, New York, New York 10020 • Text copyright © 2005 by Dan Shaughnessy • Illustrations copyright © 2005 by C. F. Payne • All rights reserved, including the right of reproduction in whole or in part in any form. • SIMON & SCHUSTER BOOKS FOR YOUNG READERS is a trademark of Simon & Schuster, Inc. • Book design by Dan Potash • The text for this book is set in Lo-Type. • The illustrations for this book are rendered in mixed media. • All newspaper images and clippings in this book are used for illustrative purposes and are created for this book only. • Manufactured in the United States of America
2 4 6 8 10 9 7 5 3 1
Library of Congress Cataloging-in-Publication Data • Shaughnessy, Dan. • The legend of the curse of the Bambino / Dan Shaughnessy ; illustrated by C. F. Payne.—1st ed. • p. cm. • "A Paula Wiseman book." • ISBN 0-689-87235-6 • 1. Boston Red Sox (Baseball team)—History—Juvenile literature. 2. New York Yankees (Baseball team)—History—Juvenile literature. 3. Ruth, Babe, 1895–1948—Juvenile literature. I. Payne, C. F., ill. II. Title. • GV875.B62S523 2005 • 796.357'64'0974461—dc22 • 2004000774